G

Don't
Call
That
Man!

Don't

Call That Man!

*A Survival Guide
to Letting Go*

Rhonda Findling

New York

Library of Congress Cataloging-in-Publication Data

Findling, Rhonda.
     Don't call that man!   :   a survival guide to letting
   go   /   Rhonda Findling.
          p.   cm.
     Previously published: Palo Alto, Calif.   :   KMK
     Associates, 1996
     ISBN 0-7868-8427-4
     1. Single women—United States—Psychology.
   2. Man-woman relationships—United States.
   3. Separation (Psychology)—United States.
   4. Dating (Social customs)—United States.   I. Title.
   HQ800.2.F45   1999
   646.7'7—dc21   99-17451
                                                         CIP

FIRST EDITION

10   9   8   7   6   5   4   3   2   1

I dedicate this book to the memory of my grandmother
Sally Porter Hassenbein

and to

Zachary, Samantha, and Madison

CONTENTS

ACKNOWLEDGMENTS

Although I am very grateful to the many people who have been supportive and helpful during the creation and development of this book, I would like to especially thank my mother, Anita Weinstein, who nurtured my creativity and self-expression as a child and encouraged the development of my talents and ambitions as an adult; my brother and friend, Drew Findling, who always brings happiness, fun, and laughter into my life; my friend and professional colleague Terry Janetatos for her support and loyalty throughout the years of our friendship and working together; Cyndi Harper-Deiters, Margot Saraceno, Lauren Field, and my sister-in-law, Beth Findling, for their support and for being there to cheer me on throughout my long, hard journey as a writer; and Raquel Hagood, who did a wonderful job typing and formatting my final manuscript and teaching me about my computer.

I would also like to express my deepest gratitude to my agent, Jillian Manus, for discovering and believing in my book; and my editor at Hyperion, Jennifer Morgan, for her belief in my book as well, and for her enthusiasm, patience, and support.

Why Not Call That Man?

Letting go of someone you love is one of the most painful feelings human beings can experience. Letting go means suffering and heartache. It means losing love, and love is the highest form of happiness known to mankind.

Letting go of love is the inspiration of much of our present-day culture. Just listen to the top ten songs on the radio. Almost all are about yearning and longing for someone loved and lost: "I Can't Live If Living Is Without You," "The Way We Were," "You Just Keep Me Hanging On."

Most of the jazz ballads sung by the great female singers (Sarah Vaughan, Billie Holiday) are about love and loss—"My Man," "The Man That Got Away."

Popular movies tell stories of women's inability to let go. *Fatal Attraction* was about a woman who became a psychotic murderer due to her obsession with a married man who rejected her. François Truffaut's *The Story of Adele H*. concerns a woman who went insane after losing a man she was in love with.

Likewise, television and theater are filled with tales of people unable to recover from loss. In the Broadway show *Sunset Boulevard*, Norma Desmond shoots her lover, Joe, because he is going to leave her. Both daytime and evening soap operas are filled with story lines of people who spend an entire television season pursuing someone who's rejected them. Daytime talk shows have an endless string of obsessed guests who can't let go.

Newspapers are filled with stories of people who can't let go no matter what the cost. Perhaps if Jean Harris had been able to mourn and grieve and work through her rage at Herman Tarnower (Dr. Scarsdale) for betraying her, she wouldn't have killed him in one of the most notorious cases of the 70s.

And if Monica Lewinsky had been able to work through all her feelings about the ending of her relationship with President Clinton with a skilled psychotherapist instead of Linda Tripp, then the course of American history might have taken a completely different turn!

So, how do I know so much about the process of letting go? I went through this experience myself.

A few years ago, I fell in love with a handsome, charismatic, articulate, and mystical man. During our relationship, I became emotionally dependent on him. He taught me much about spirituality. He was loving and supportive. I thought he understood me in a way no one else did. However, when I expressed my desire for more commitment from him, he left.

Looking back, I strongly feel that his sudden and almost cruel rejection was caused by his intimacy problems. When I first met him, he told me he had not had a relationship in more than seven years, and was not looking for a commitment. I fell in love with him any-way, hoping I would be the exception. Despite my professional insight as a psychotherapist, I was still left wounded and devastated. I had to learn the arduous process of letting go so I could recover and move on with my life.

At the same time, I was treating several women who were also having a hard time letting go of relationships that had ended. I decided to start a support/psychotherapy group titled Don't Call That Man! I did workshops in the community and soon found myself on radio and television talk shows as a "relationship expert." It seemed this was my path.

From my own personal experience and professional work, I learned how deeply abandonment and rejection in adulthood can wound. The pain of rejection can reach into the very core of one's being. A woman can become so fixated on a man who rejects her that she is consumed by her rage and desire for him. I've known women to lose their health, money, jobs, children—even go to jail—because of their preoccupation with a man who got away. I've had women come to my support groups and workshops who were on the brink of suicide because of a breakup and their inability to move on.

Women have come a long way financially but still have a lot of work to do to become more emotionally independent. Too many financially self-sufficient women stay in emotionally and physically abusive relationships because they are terrified of letting go. They would rather cling to a man who beats, humiliates, or rejects them than risk the terror of being alone.

In the following chapters, I will teach you to develop the inner resources and skills to let go, so you don't destroy your life for the sake of romantic love and fear of loneliness. The writing exercises will give you a chance to express and experience your feelings—an essential part of the healing process.

This book, the writing exercises, and the Ten-Step Program evolved from my work with the women in workshops and the Don't Call That Man! support/psychotherapy group. Although the majority of the women in the groups and workshops were going through breakups, some were in relationships with unavailable men. These women were looking for the strength and support to leave. Other women felt they were acting too clingy and desperate in their present relationships and wanted more insight into their behavior.

The case scenarios I discuss in this book are based on female patients I've worked with and people I've known socially who have struggled with the problem of letting go. All names or identifying characteristics have been changed.

If you are in a relationship and find yourself wanting to call your man too much out of anxiety or panic that he is going to leave or lose interest, then you can use this book as well. Use the writing exercises, The Ten-Step Program, and the information here to work on your own issues so you do not come across as needy and desperate, which can turn off even the healthiest man.

If you are going through a breakup, you can use this book to help your recovery. By following the advice to control yourself to keep from running after your ex, you will recover from the loss with your pride and self-esteem intact. You will not only survive, you will triumph. You may even go on to find a new love—one who will always be there for you.

There really is life after that man!

ONE

Breaking the
Compulsive Cycle

Sheila, an attractive twenty-seven-year-old computer programmer, sat in her apartment staring at the telephone. She yearned to call Tony, a handsome life insurance salesman she had been dating for the past six months.

Initially, Sheila had thought Tony was perfect. He was charming, ambitious, and attentive. Eventually, after a romantic dinner in an expensive French restaurant, Sheila got up the nerve to ask Tony about their future. Her heart sank when he said he did not see himself marrying her. He suggested they should start dating other people. Hurt and angry that he didn't want to marry her, Sheila told Tony she didn't think they should see each other anymore.

Now Sheila felt alone and desperate. She wanted to be with Tony on any terms—his terms. She couldn't bear the thought of life without him. She felt as if it was all her fault. If only she could undo that conversation, maybe they would still be together. She had to speak to him.

She dialed his number, hoping he was home. His answering machine came on. She hung up. She decided to wait and call later. She tried to keep busy doing housework, but she couldn't stop thinking of him, so she went back and dialed again. Again the machine answered. She started dialing every fifteen minutes for more than two hours. She knew she was out of control. She was like a junkie writhing in pain for a fix, but she couldn't seem to help herself. She couldn't bear the thought of not seeing Tony anymore.

We can all relate to Sheila and how she feels because we have all been through this emotional scenario to some degree. The symptoms are painfully familiar: the fear of losing control, the yearning to hear his voice again. You know your behavior is out of control, yet you are unable to put the brakes on the continuous stream of telephone calls. You don't know what to do.

What is it that makes us feel our emotional stability is too shaken that we will go to any lengths to get a man to come back? Why can't we just let go?

Let's look at a few components that lead women down this path. Abandonment is among one of our most primal fears. To be abandoned as a child is to die. A child cannot survive without the nurturing of adults. Depending on our individual histories, that fear remains within us to some degree.

As adults, if we are abandoned by someone to whom we look for love and support, our childhood fear of abandonment is triggered. The result is an activation of the childhood fear, which, coupled with the present threat of abandonment, can generate intense fear and panic. Our ability to reason rationally may be so affected that all we experience is the terror of the abandonment.

When we feel abandoned, we can experience panic over suddenly being alone, together with a feeling of rejection. These painful feelings can trigger clinging. Clinging is any behavior that demonstrates holding on, not letting go. This can be exemplified by activities ranging from a compulsive phone call to showing up at his apartment or place of work without advance warning. Or writing him a continuous stream of letters or E-mails even though he hasn't responded to any of your previous contacts.

When a woman is in a clinging state, she can become so desperate she will resort to behavior that is humiliating and bordering on masochistic. Nancy was so upset when her boyfriend wouldn't see her anymore that she went to his house, fell to her knees, and begged him to take her back. She told me that when she was actually groveling on her knees, she cared nothing for her pride or self-respect—all that mattered was her belief that she couldn't live without him.

Marcy went to her ex-boyfriend's apartment building and told the doorman to ring his bell upstairs. The ex-boyfriend responded that he didn't want her to come up. She became distraught and told the doorman she wouldn't leave the lobby until her boyfriend came down to speak to her. The doorman threatened to call the police, but in her desperation, she wouldn't leave. Eventually, the police did arrive and Marcy skulked away, terribly humiliated and ashamed.

The pain and humiliation these women endured is not uncommon. Many women, even those you wouldn't suspect perhaps because of their success, fame, and/or beauty, have experienced what Marcy, Nancy, and Sheila went through.

Wanting to compulsively call your ex or cling to him when you know the relationship is over can serve to mask or anesthetize your feelings of loneliness, hurt, and pain. The same concept applies to women who are presently in a relationship or dating someone new, and are afraid they'll never hear from him again. When you compulsively call a man because of your own fear of abandonment, there can be a pleasurable rush of adrenaline with the anticipation of seeing him or just hearing his voice. But this rush is just a temporary fix. The true road to emotional freedom is to feel the pain of his absence and work through the pain by yourself or with support.

If there is any hope of the relationship being salvaged, or you want to keep the relationship you presently have, then it's important to remember that desperate, clinging behavior causes most men to distance themselves even further. Acting desperate and needy makes you look like you feel unlovable and that you're grateful *any* man is paying attention to you.

If a man has his own issues about intimacy and closeness, your clinging will make him feel closed in and claustrophobic because he feels he has no room to breathe from your relentlessly trying to get him to prove that he's not going to leave you. Your clinging also makes you look emotionally hungry, making him feel that he'll have to endlessly supply you with the reassuring love you're in such desperate need of, which seems like a large job for anyone.

It's human nature to have a hard time falling in love with someone who's bombarding you with phone calls. A desperate woman doesn't leave a man a chance to long and yearn for her. She's so available, he doesn't have the space to fantasize about her or miss her, which unfortunately is sometimes what falling in love is all about.

Desperately clinging can lead to a vicious cycle. The more he distances himself, the more you cling. He distances further, you cling more desperately.

Even with this insight and knowledge, the urge to cling can be irresistible. You know with your rational mind that your behavior isn't appropriate, but you are driven by a compulsion you feel you can't control. You feel actual discomfort when you don't carry out the compulsive act.

What is the healthy thing to do when you're having a compulsive, irresistible urge to call a man?

First, give yourself permission to experience the tension and your feelings. Tolerate them until they pass—and they will pass. Feelings are just temporary. That's the trick—to feel your feelings, and to not act them out. It will take a great deal of self-discipline and work. It's easier to feel something, give in to your feelings, and act out. Holding in your feelings, experiencing the feelings, and not acting them out is known as *containing* your feelings.

A warning: You will feel tension when you are in the process of containing your feelings. You'll probably want relief from the tension because you'll actually be uncomfortable. This discomfort will drive you to want to call him, because what you want is immediate gratification from the release of tension. Remember, however, the anguish and pain you may have to go through if he rejects you, or if you don't get the response you yearn for.

Toni, one of the women in my group, had a list of friends she would call when she was overwhelmed by the urge of wanting to contact her ex-boyfriend. Helen, another group member, would go to a gym and work out when she wanted to make a call. If the gym was closed, she'd just go out and run. Barbara went to the movies. Soon, everyone in my support group had a list of things to do when they got the overpowering impulse to call that man.

It is of paramount importance for you to understand that just because you contain your feelings, you should not prevent yourself from expressing them to others. People such as a trusted nonjudgmental friend or support group can be especially helpful, as is a qualified therapist. If you absolutely must wing it alone, then do so with the assurance that other women have done it, and so can you. It's not the best situation, but certainly possible to do.

The whole point of resisting the urge to call a man you have broken up with and share your feelings with him is to avoid the risk of getting rejected, hurt, or humiliated. Every time you get rejected, you reinforce any feelings of unlovability or desperation you might be struggling with.

And even if he does respond to your call positively, you may feel momentarily comforted and closer to him, but soon the anguish *will return*, because you're still not together and then you'll have to work through your feelings of loss again, doubling your amount of work.

Going through the pain without him may seem like passing through a crucible of fire, but if you don't call that man, you'll feel triumphant and confident of your own inner resources.

TWO

Mourning and Grieving

When a relationship has ended, or you see your man distancing or pulling away from you, it's a *loss*, even if it's a temporary loss. Whenever there is a loss, you have to feel the pain of the loss.

I hate saying this to my patients because I don't like telling people they have to feel pain in order to get better and move on. Unfortunately, it's true. The only way to get better is to free yourself—not be imprisoned by your love—and feel all of your feelings.

The process of going through a loss is called *mourning*. It is a complicated process that includes many feelings—grief, longing and yearning, hopelessness, anger, apathy, sadness, and despair.

Grief is a painful, even agonizing, feeling, but a necessary one to acknowledge the pain of loss. Denying the existence of the pain may lead you to call him compulsively, causing you to be unable to move on and love someone else. When you grieve, you may be grieving for the loss of your ex's company, making love with him, his touch and comfort, the fantasy of a future together, children you might have had together, the pleasure and happiness you experienced together.

There may be times when you will feel consumed by the grief, afraid you will never get over your pain, but only by experiencing these feelings fully can you move beyond the pain and sadness. You have to embrace it. If you give a feeling full expression, it diminishes and brings about transformation. The feeling *will* subside. It will *not* go on forever.

Remember, grief has its own rhythms. You cannot decide, "Okay, I'm going to grieve now." You have to feel grief when it arises.

Stages of Loss

When mourning the loss of a man you were in love with, you will go through four stages. You may not pass through each stage in order, and sometimes the stages overlap. The following stages are based on the five stages of death and dying delineated in Dr. Elizabeth Kübler-Ross's famous 1969 book *On Death and Dying*.

Denial is the first stage. You do not want to face the reality that he's gone, that he rejected you, or that he's done something awful to provoke you to break up with him. You are in emotional shock. You may even feel numb.

It's important during the stage of denial to try and cope with reality. If you pretend everything is still the same and pursue a man you just broke up with, you may end up feeling even more hurt and humiliated. This is a good time to turn to your support system for help in facing the truth and the reality of the situation.

DON'T CALL THAT MAN!

Anger is the second stage. You are facing reality now and feeling enraged at him for betraying you, hurting you, abandoning you. Unresolved anger at others who have hurt you in the past (parents, ex-boyfriends) may reemerge now.

However, it's important to work through your anger without contacting your ex. Don't use your anger as an excuse to confront him, tell him off, or even worse, become violent. Acting out your anger with your ex won't help the situation. In fact, it might make it worse. Most people don't respond well to aggressive confrontation, so you probably won't get the response that you're looking for. You may feel better momentarily but his response to your anger could result in your feeling more hurt, abandoned, or angry. Instead, share your feelings of anger with members of your support system. You can also work through your anger by working out, playing sports, writing or other creative activities.

The third and fourth stages are *depression* and *despair*. These are the most difficult stages. The excitement and drama of the breakup is over and you're left with the emptiness of the loss. Any past abandonments you may have struggled with, which you might have also experienced in the anger stage, could come up for you now, which could contribute to your feelings of sadness and depression. This can be a painful time for you but it is necessary for you to go through this stage in order to move on to a new relationship. If you stay in denial, you will remain haunted by your past. However, if you're feeling so depressed that you are having difficulty functioning (you stop working, eating, sleeping), you might be clinically depressed and it may be necessary for you to consult a medical doctor or psychiatrist.

Again, it is important that you don't call that man during this stage. This is a difficult and vulnerable time for you and you cannot take the risk of his acting distant or rejecting you because it could cause you to feel even more abandoned, leading to further depression and despair. This is an especially important time to call on your support system for emotional nurturing. Try to be self-comforting while you bite the bullet and struggle through the pain. Although this stage may feel overwhelming, remember that time heals all wounds and your feelings of sadness and despair will come to an end. You will eventually move to the final stage: acceptance.

Acceptance is when you begin to pull your life back together again. You're not so preoccupied with your ex anymore. You start thinking about new men and you want to start dating. This can be a tricky time though, because you may want to call your ex just to show him you're over him. But don't give in and call, because you may not get the response you want and then you'll feel let down and disappointed. Or worse, your old feelings for him may resurface and then you're in a setback and you'll have to start mourning him all over again!!!

Another important part of the mourning and grieving process is feeling all your feelings, including the good ones. Don't be ashamed of having loving, romantic feelings toward your ex even though the relationship is over or he has really hurt you. This is only natural. There were qualities about him that you loved or enjoyed, or you would never have gotten involved or fallen in love with him.

You must also yearn and long for your ex. Don't be ashamed. These are just feelings—you are not acting them out, you are feeling them.

Gratitude is another feeling you may need to express. You may be holding on to the relationship because you feel grateful about something he did for you. Vivian was grateful to her boyfriend for helping to financially support her through law school. Barbara was grateful to her boyfriend for being emotionally supportive when she went through a painful divorce. Both of them needed to express these feelings in the group because they kept focusing on how wonderful their respective exes were, although the relationships were over.

You may even experience feelings of envy toward your ex. He may have some quality you admire and wish you had. Betty admired her boyfriend Paul's ability to socialize with people. She often watched him at parties as he engaged and connected with others with such ease.

You will undoubtedly feel anger and rage at your ex for abandoning you, treating you unfairly, betraying, rejecting, or abusing you. Working through these feelings and not allowing them to take over is paramount to getting over him.

The key to this process is *NOT* to call him even when you are feeling such powerful feelings. You must use this time to emotionally distance and disconnect from him. If you call him to express and share your feelings, and he doesn't appreciate what you are going through and rejects or emotionally dismisses you, you will feel a hundred times worse. This will contaminate the healing process and the hard work you have done to mourn and let go of him.

Instead, share these feeling with someone else—a therapist, a supportive friend, or a support group. Make sure it's someone you feel safe with. Having a witness to this experience of love, pain, sadness, and yearning makes the process of letting go more meaningful. However, there may be times when there will be no one available to share these powerful feelings with—you will have to feel them by yourself. When it hits in the middle of the night, you can't call people and wake them at four in the morning (unless you have incredibly understanding friends!). Instead, you can cry by yourself. You can develop the skills of soothing and nurturing yourself, which will be discussed in chapter three.

Betty and Tim had been engaged for six months when Tim told Betty he didn't know if he could marry her. Betty was devastated. They had dated for more than a year before getting engaged. Tim had moved to New York from Greece to study for a master's degree in engineering. A year after he came to New York, he met Betty in a nightclub. After the first date, they began spending most of their free time together. When Tim's family found out about their engagement, they became angry because they wanted him to marry a Greek woman. They threatened to disown Tim if he went through with the marriage. Tim decided he could not give up his family and told Betty he could not go through with the wedding.

Betty was enraged at Tim for his inability to stand up to his family and his betrayal of their love and future together. Although she was able to function at her job as a credit investigator, Betty was becoming severely depressed. She decided to seek therapy. When she came to see me, we discussed her symptoms of depression as well as her inability to completely let go of Tim.

On occasion, Tim still called Betty, though he had not changed his decision about marriage. This was making Betty even more confused. In therapy, she decided she wanted to make a complete break from Tim.

Betty spent the first few therapy sessions getting in touch with her grief, and crying. She also spoke about all the things she missed about Tim: his calling her twice a day when they were dating, their sexual relationship, even the ordinary routine of going to the movies together. She especially mourned the loss of the future they would have shared. She cried over the wedding they had planned. They had even picked out their children's names. This was the most painful part for her.

She then expressed her rage at Tim for rejecting and abandoning her. She acknowledged her gradual insight into why he did this, including his attachment to his family and his inability to emotionally separate from them.

During this time, Tim called her once more. Because she was feeling emotionally stronger, Betty told him not to call anymore. She said it only confused her since they had no future together. After asserting herself, she felt less like a victim—her depression lifted. She was able to talk about the good times they had together, how he had financially helped when she went back to graduate school. She was able to get in touch with her feelings of gratitude toward him. She remembered how loving and affectionate he could be with her.

Despite the good feelings Betty was having about Tim, she was able to contain these feelings within the therapy. She did not call him to share these positive loving feelings because she knew it would cause further confusion.

When Betty started to date again, she sometimes compared other men to Tim. This would cause her to have strong longings and yearnings again because she was afraid she would never meet someone she felt as comfortable with as Tim. As she continued to work through her grief, her feelings about Tim began to diminish—in a year she could think about him without pain or remorse. She now saw the whole thing as a learning experience. She felt emotionally free enough to become seriously involved with another man. She was not afraid of risking another relationship because she knew she was capable of loving and, if necessary, working through loss again.

What can you do to facilitate the process of mourning?

- To relieve anger, you can do physical exercise. (Running, playing tennis, working out, wrestling, kickboxing, or taking martial arts classes are great!) Any activity where you can physically release your anger and discharge tension from your body will help.

- Express your feelings through creativity: write prose, poetry, lyrics to songs. Paint, sing, dance.

- Verbalize your feelings. Keep talking to people in your support system about your feelings.

- Write a letter of good-bye to your relationship. Write this letter as if your ex could hear the letter being read. Say everything that needs to be said. Let your feelings come as you write. Cry while writing the letter. But *don't send it*. It can be a powerful experience to read this letter to a trusted friend, someone who can bear witness to your feelings. You might want to save the letter to look at after time has passed, or tear it up as a symbol of ending your connection with him.

The act of ritual can also facilitate healing and the movement through the mourning process.

Donna was upset because she was legally separated from Mark and having a particularly hard time emotionally letting go of the relationship. On the evening of her birthday, she was afraid she didn't have the willpower to not call Mark, so she decided to go out with her friends Linda and Susan. The three friends commemorated the end of Donna's relationship with Mark by driving past the restaurant where the couple used to go every Friday. As the women sat in the parking lot, Donna related her past experiences with Mark.

Later, the three women drove to the beach, where Donna took off the ring Mark had given her and threw it into the ocean. She cried afterward. Linda and Susan were supportive and compassionate, sharing their own stories of loss. Finally, they went to a fancy restaurant to celebrate Donna's birthday, the end of her relationship with Mark, and her newfound freedom. They feasted on rich pastries and coffee, sharing stories about past relationships and adventures with men, laughing and crying until the café closed.

When Donna came to see me for her next therapy session, she said she felt much better and was able to accept the ending of the relationship.

You can plan rituals with friends or do them by yourself. They are just another way for you to express the change and transformation in your life.

The most important element in all forms of mourning is sharing your story with others. Whether you are telling your therapist, your best friend, or your mother,

when you tell your story, you no longer feel alone or
isolated. You feel understood, connected. Often the
more you talk about what happened to you, the more
distance you put between yourself and the pain.

With the presence of a compassionate and caring
person, you can share and communicate joy and sor-
row, healing any trauma or wound.

✐ Writing Exercises

These writing exercises are designed to help you let go
of the past. You need to write out the answers, then
think about them. This is processing your responses.
Exploring your feelings as you answer the questions is
part of the healing process.

• Have you been experiencing feelings of sadness or
despair?

• Have you been feeling anger and rage at your ex?
What did your ex do to cause you to feel angry?

• What kinds of things do you think you can do to
express feelings of anger or grief in a healthy, con-
structive way?

• Do you have someone you can share your feelings
with when you are sad or angry? Describe that person.

• If you are overwhelmed in the middle of the night with feelings of grief or anger, what can you do for yourself to calm down?

• What imaginative way can you think of to commemorate the ending of your relationship in a ceremony? Write about it, no matter how outlandish you might think it is.

THREE

Recovering from Rejection

Just because you're mourning and grieving, it doesn't mean you have to wallow in pain all day! It's also very important to nurture yourself during times of loss and rejection. You need to restore yourself to the way you were before the emotional injury of his rejection. How do you do this? You must start soothing yourself immediately. Do whatever makes you feel good for the next few days until the initial pain begins to subside. Here are just a few suggestions on how to indulge yourself:

Get your hair done. Sign up for that course you always wanted to take. Visit your family out of state. Go to Paris. Go to the movies all day long. Go to a concert. Get a massage. Have a facial. Go shopping. Join a health spa where you can work out. Take personal time off from your job. Go off your diet and eat desserts all day long. Visit all your friends and talk about your ex. Talk on the phone all night. Hire a baby-sitter for your kids and go out dancing.

The sky's the limit! Gratify yourself. Do things that

bring you pleasure. This is self-care. Think of it as if you were on a vacation. Try not to make many demands on yourself. Keep your life as stress-free as possible during this time. The whole point is to get through the next few days so the initial suffering from the loss or rejection starts to diminish.

Don't use drugs or drink alcohol during this time. They may numb the pain temporarily but you are just putting off the inevitable pain of loss you will have to face. You need to stay sober and centered now. And you don't need the additional problem of chemical or alcohol addiction.

After a week, you may have to cut down on some of these pleasurable activities because if you keep eating desserts all day, taking time off your job, and shopping, you may be out of a job, overweight, and deep in debt by the time you're over your ex. There are many ways to continue healing yourself that are not addictive and eventually self-destructive.

Individual psychotherapy, group psychotherapy, self-help groups (twelve-step programs), massage, reflexology, astrology, hypnotherapy, bibliotherapy (reading books), prayer circles, acupuncture, meditation. The list goes on and on.

Remember, don't call that man who rejected you. You will only reinjure yourself, like pulling a scab off a wound. It will ruin all the hard work you've done up until now. If it is impossible for you to function, and you're having a hard time getting up to go to work, feeling deeply depressed, and/or having suicidal thoughts, then you may be clinically depressed and you may need professional help and medication. Don't be ashamed if you need to resort to medication, because loss and rejection can bring up trauma from your past, which you may need professional help with to recover from and get through.

Support

While you are working on restoring and healing yourself, it's essential for you to have a support system. You need friends you can talk to when you have an urge to call your ex, or you are feeling depressed and hopeless.

It's important that people in your support system do not criticize or shame you or make you feel worse. People in your support system should be emotionally supportive. It would be helpful if they are some of the following things: sensitive, nonjudgmental, nurturing, compassionate, emotionally available, encouraging, validating, and trustworthy.

Try to work on having three people in your life you can call on whenever you have an urge to call your ex. Carry their phone numbers around with you. Your support system could be made up of friends, family members, coworkers, professionals, clergy—whoever you feel safe with. Be selective with whom you trust to tell your problems to though. It's good to have a number of friends to depend on because you don't want to be too draining on just one person. Keep working on and putting energy into increasing your support network.

Having a support system not only helps you to not contact that man, but it helps you feel less isolated and loved. Knowing that there are people other than your ex who care about you makes you feel emotionally connected to others, which will help prevent loneliness, depression, and feelings of desperation.

Amy and Tom had been friends for almost a year. Amy

had been supportive of Tom when he ended his marriage, and Tom had been there for Amy when she and her fiancé broke up. This was the first time in their friendship they were both without a partner. Sometimes Amy caught Tom looking at her dreamily when they met for lunch, which he usually initiated. He often called her in the evening just to see how she was doing and to talk about his day. One time he bought her a book of poems.

Amy had a feeling that Tom was interested in her romantically and thought that maybe they could explore the possibility of dating. The next time they met for lunch, Amy told Tom she was attracted to him and was wondering about his feelings about her. Tom looked stunned and told Amy that he thought of her as a sister and didn't think they would make a good couple. He also told her that he had begun dating a new woman who he thought he might be in love with. Humiliated and hurt, Amy finished the lunch quickly and excused herself.

Enraged at Tom for sending her double messages and rejecting her, Amy thought that their friendship was now ruined. But despite her anger, Amy still hoped that Tom would call to tell her he had made a mistake and that he did have romantic feelings for her. A week passed and he never called. Amy realized she was more attached to Tom than she'd thought and became depressed. She began to have urges to call him but felt it would be too humiliating and that the healthiest thing to do was to move on.

That night she made a schedule for the entire week so that she wouldn't sit around depressed, waiting for the phone to ring. During the day she'd go to work, but in the evenings she would stay busy so that she wouldn't miss Tom's phone calls.

On Monday she went for a massage. Afterward she went to an art house movie she wanted to see but had put off. On Tuesday she went to dinner with a friend she hadn't seen in a long time. She met another friend for dessert afterward. On Wednesday she went shopping and bought a dress she'd been dying to get. When she got home she started to feel the pain of Tom's absence and rejection, and called friends who were home that night to discuss and talk to them about what had happened with Tom. On Thursday she went to see her therapist, whom she hadn't seen in two years. She took two vacation days and left the city that weekend to visit her sister and nieces.

When she got back from her trip, Amy felt a little better. She had spent a lot of money in the past week and had to be more careful with her budget now. But she decided she would stay in therapy until she recovered from Tom's rejection and would visit her friends a lot for the next couple of weeks. She also decided to start an acting course where she thought she might work out some of her feelings; it could also be an avenue for her to meet new people. Besides, secretly she had always wanted to be an actress and she thought this was a good time for her to pursue one of her dreams that she had always put off.

✎ Writing Exercises

• Does the current loss and rejection you are experiencing bring up past rejections? What were those rejections?

• Describe your feelings toward the person you lost or who rejected you.

• What things could you do for yourself right now that would ease the pain?

• Describe your lovable and likable traits.

• Describe and list some of the people in your life who love and like you. Include those you know are grateful that you are in their life.

• Are you giving the person who rejected you too much power? List some of their negative traits.

• List some healing activities you can do this week
that will make you feel better.

FOUR

Inadequate Fathering

Yearning for a Fantasy Father

If you are having a difficult time letting go of a relationship when it's over, or constantly calling your present boyfriend because you are afraid he's going to leave you, then you may be suffering from inadequate fathering. So many girls are growing up without fathers in their households, or with fathers who are only in their lives sporadically, that it is easy to see how women can suffer from a lack of father nurturing.

As dismal as these facts are, absence is not the only way your father may not have been there for you. He may have been emotionally unavailable. This could have been due to addiction to sex, work, drugs, or alcohol. He may have had problems with relating, or a style of relating that was very distancing. He may have been depressed or physically ill. He may have been a very self-absorbed man.

It is important to mention here that emotional unavailability is considered emotional abandonment, and therefore should be treated as a loss. Emotional unavailability can be just as traumatizing as physical desertion.

Abusing or humiliating your mother in front of you is also inadequate fathering, because, as a little girl, you identify with your mother and internalize the way she is treated by your father. Any kind of fighting or spouse abuse in front of a child is stressful and traumatizing to the child. At those moments, your father was not thinking of you or the long-term damaging effects the abuse would have on you.

Of course, if your father physically, sexually, or emotionally abused you, he was not fathering you. This is the most extreme case of a father who is so preoccupied with his own needs and problems. He is completely incapable of relating to his daughter's needs for fathering.

You may have had inadequate fathering if you had a father:

- who was overly preoccupied with himself or his problems

- whose needs always came before yours

- who sexually, emotionally, or physically abused you

- who physically and/or financially deserted you and your family

You were entitled to a father who was:

- empathic

DON'T CALL THAT MAN!

- understanding

- interested in you

- understandable (not confusing and full of double messages)

- respectful of you

- able to take you seriously

- willing to financially provide for you while you were growing up

When I was twelve years old, my parents divorced. Although my father was working, he left to "do his own thing" and did not pay child support. He left my mother, brother, and me stranded in a house that was being foreclosed on. The car was repossessed because my father did not pay the bills. My mother was a housewife and had no marketable skills. We were impoverished. Despite my mother's attempts through the courts, my father was able to work the system, rarely paying support. He never made any attempt to pay for any part of my higher education. I was persistent, held down three jobs at a time, and finished college.

Even now, as an adult and a professional woman, I still find his selfishness and lack of paternal instinct and caring difficult to comprehend. When I began to date, I chose handsome, charming, self-absorbed men like my father to become involved with. Until I got into therapy and worked through my feelings about my father's abandonment, I wasted a lot of time and energy on men who were incapable of healthy relationships.

Inadequate Fathering and
Your Relationships

If you also grew up with inadequate
fathering, it could be affecting your
relationships with men in various
ways:

- You may get panicky when you feel a man distancing or leaving you. This terror stems from
unconscious memories of your father's abandonment, which you have not psychologically
worked through. This fear of being left or
rejected could lead to your acting desperate
and clingy to the extent of humiliating, self-
destructive behavior.

- You may get involved with men who are similar
to your father, trying to rewrite and resolve history. It is like squeezing blood from a stone—
you are trying to get love from a man who may
be emotionally incapable of giving love, just like
your father. The sad reality is that you can find a
million men like your father, but you will never
get the fathering you needed when you were a
child. It's too late. Repeating the trauma over
and over won't give you the fathering you
needed. Only you can heal the wound now as
an adult.

- You may get involved with men like your father
because you have not emotionally separated
from him (even though you may not even be in
contact with him!). By getting involved with

men like him, the little-girl part of you can stay attached to the father of her childhood. It seems ironic that you would have difficulty emotionally separating from someone who wasn't even there for you earlier. You may still be clinging to an image of the father you yearned for but never had.

Without emotionally separating from this image, you will have unrealistic expectations of men or make unrealistic demands upon them. For instance, you might expect a man you are dating to pay some of your bills or buy you material things. This is acting out your yearning to be taken care of the way you wanted your father to care for you as a child. Such entitlement on your part can turn a man off. He is looking for a girlfriend or a partner, not a daughter!

You may expect unconditional love from men because you feel that a man could not possibly leave you if he loved you that way. This could lead to your not accepting his decision to end a relationship, resulting in your having a hard time letting go. This is the path to that same old self-destructive behavior.

Unrealistic expectations of unconditional love could also cause you to feel as if you can do anything to him without consequence. Of course, this is a completely unrealistic assumption for an adult. There are consequences for behavior. If you do things to make him angry or turn him off, he could reject or leave you. He is not your father or the father you wish you had. A man will stay with you because he wants to, not because he owes it to you. Your father owed it to you to stay with you throughout your childhood; this sense of entitlement should be directed toward your father, not your lover!

If you find yourself acting out in any of these ways, you may need to resolve your father issues to prevent sabotaging, ruining, or at the very least lessening your chances for a successful relationship.

Letting Go of the Little Girl

So how do you emotionally separate from your father? How do you recover from the pain and anguish of not getting the love you needed and yearned for?

The key to letting go of the father of your past and recovering from what you didn't get as a child is *grieving* and *mourning.* You have to grieve and mourn for the little girl who didn't get the love and emotional sustenance she needed and was entitled to from her father. You have to grieve and mourn for the romantic hero-father you idealized as a little girl, but who disappointed you. He was the man who got away!

Once you get in touch with feelings of rejection, deprivation, and loss, a lot of pain, anger, and rage can surface. It is usually better to feel such strong emotions with a psychotherapist, support group, or a supportive friend, although it is possible to do it alone. Often you can work through grief and mourning through creativity—famous artists, writers, and musicians admittedly work through deep feelings in their work.

And most important of all, you need to get in touch with your love for your father. All little girls love and adore their daddies. I did. Passionately. In fact, I was a daddy's girl, which is probably why I was so devastated by his abandonment.

It is your love and adoration for your father and his not returning it in the way you needed that caused the wounding. This is where your heart is broken, where the healing needs to be done. Even as we grow older, we sometimes still secretly yearn for our fathers to admire and love us. Elyce Wakerman, in her book *Father Loss* (Bantam Doubleday Dell), describes it perfectly:

> *I stood before the mirror, a fifteen-year-old girl, and belted out a song. Alone in that adolescent haven, my bedroom, I shed the self-effacing posture that is my daily accessory, throw back my shoulders, toss back my hair, and sing my heart out. "I'm the greatest star. I am by far, but no one knows it." Behind the singer's reflection, there is a smiling audience of one, who, unlike all others, appreciates my star-like qualities. Here in the cherished privacy of my room, I entertain a fantasy and acknowledge before the mirror my longing for his applause. Sometimes, now that I am grown and speaking of such things, I still find myself wondering, at the end of the chapter, for instance, "Daddy are you clapping?"*

It is only when you have consciously gotten in touch with all of your feelings for your father as an adult that you can start to emotionally separate from the father of your past. You can go on to view him more realistically as neither monster nor romantic hero. You may even come to realize that he was unable to father you adequately because he lacked good parenting. He probably didn't get the love he needed as a little boy. It was never you—you were never unlovable or undeserving of love. It was his stuff. It is when you really get this that your life can change.

It wasn't until Linda's relationship with Ivan almost ended that issues about her father began to surface. Linda had been dating Ivan for a year when she came to see me. Ivan was a noncustodial divorced father of two little girls. He worked five days a week in construction and saw his daughters on the weekends. Linda worked as a secretary and wanted to get married and start a family. Everything went well until Ivan's ex-wife asked him to spend more time with his daughters while she recovered from an operation. Linda tried to be understanding of Ivan's added responsibilities, but soon found herself consumed by jealousy and anger. She began calling Ivan more often, even though she could tell he was getting irritated. Eventually, Linda was dropping by Ivan's house unannounced. He was usually too busy with his daughters to spend time with her, which led to Linda feeling rejected.

One night they had a terrible argument, with Linda accusing Ivan of not having enough time for her. Ivan said he was feeling too stressed out and thought they should break up for a while. Devastated, Linda started taking prescription antidepressants, but felt they weren't helping her and decided to try psychotherapy. When she came to see me, Linda began to explore her past and got in touch with a lot of buried feelings about her father.

When Linda was growing up, her father worked sixteen hours a day. He was hardly ever home, and Linda spent most of her time with her mother or by herself. She had very few memories of spending quality time with her father, who had died five years before she came to see me. Linda needed to mourn the death of her father more completely, as well as the fathering she felt she never got.

She spent many sessions discussing the details of

her feelings when her father wasn't there for her. She was able to get in touch with yearnings for her father to pay attention to her. She became more aware of her envy of Ivan's relationship with his daughters. She cried through many sessions as she got in touch with her feelings of rejection and emotional abandonment by her father. She became consciously aware of how she often got involved in unrequited love relationships as a form of reenacting her relationship with her father. She also cried about his death, because there would never be a chance for them to work things out.

Ivan called Linda one evening and they decided to get together to talk. Linda told Ivan about everything she had learned from her experience in therapy. Ivan, an understanding, compassionate man, was very open to the changes Linda had made. His coping skills with the added responsibility of child care had improved, and he now had more time for a relationship. He and Linda eventually moved in together and are now thinking of getting married.

It was after doing the mourning work that Linda was freer in relating to Ivan, rather than repetitively acting out unresolved issues with her father.

When you have mourned and emotionally separated from an unhealthy relationship with your father, you can better choose a man for a relationship. You must do this mourning and grieving work so you don't spend the rest of your life repeating painful abandonment, loneliness, and suffering over and over. You must work on your father issues so that, rather than being a prisoner of your past, you will have control over your life and destiny.

✍ Writing Exercises

• Describe your father in a paragraph.

• Describe his nurturing qualities.

• Describe ways in which he may have been inadequate as a father.

• Describe what his father was like.

• Describe what his childhood was like.

• Describe ways you wish your father had been more nurturing.

• Describe ways you think you might have been deprived of fathering while growing up.

• Was your father abusive to you physically, emotionally, or otherwise? If so, write about it here.

• Was your father abusive to your mother? If so, write about it here.

• What do you dislike about your father?

• What do you admire most about your father?

• Describe your impressions of your father when you were a little girl.

• Describe your impressions of your father when you were a teenager.

• Describe ways you may need to psychologically separate from your father—that you need to work on.

• Describe ways you may be acting out your childhood attachment to your father.

• How are the men you choose to become involved with similar to your father?

• How are they different?

• What traits do you have that are similar to your father's?

• If you could have had an ideal father, what would he have been like?

• How has your relationship with your father evolved? If he's still alive, what is your relationship with him like now?

FIVE

Mothers and Men

Did you notice that the man you're having a hard time letting go of reminds you of your mother? Most women have an intense bond with their mothers. After all, most of us had women as primary caretakers from the time that we were born. So even though you fall in love with men, you may get drawn to ones who have the character traits your mother has.

Sometimes we fall in love with a man who relates to us the way our mothers did. If your mother didn't pay enough attention to you and didn't listen well, perhaps you'll get involved with a man who is a poor listener. If she was self-absorbed and put her needs before yours, then you might get involved with a man who puts his needs before yours. It's hard to let go of these men when the relationship ends because it's like letting go of your mother.

If your mother had competitive issues and was unloving, you may have felt unloved. Or if she had a lot of self-hatred and was hateful to you, you may have internalized her hatred and ended up with low self-esteem.

Often we copy the way our mothers relate to men. If she accepts abusive behavior from men, then you might tolerate abusive behavior too. If your mother is terrified of being alone and clings to her man, then you might repeat this behavior and cling to men too.

Most women love their mothers even if they are often angry or frustrated with them. If we have a more successful relationship than our mothers, we feel guilty that we're getting more love from a man than our mothers did. It hurts us to see our mothers suffer. We feel her pain as if it's happening to us. (Sometimes we don't want to leave our mother emotionally so we hold on to her by repeating her life.) We get involved with men who don't treat us right or hopeless relationships just like our mothers had with their men. We get into "go nowhere" situations that aren't successful so that we aren't happier than our mothers. If she's suffered, we copy our mother's behavior and cling to unhealthy men because our mothers did. Sometimes we hold on to our mothers by becoming attracted to and involved with men like our fathers. Sometimes we even grovel and humiliate ourselves with men because being happier and more successful than our mothers can be terrifying.

For years in my twenties I related to men the same way my mother did in my childhood. She would tolerate my father's dysfunctional, sometimes abusive behavior, then get angry and fed up and leave him, only to give him another chance when he promised he'd change . . . back and forth . . . chaotic. It took psychotherapy and work on myself to learn new ways to relate to men that were different from the way my mother had when I was a little girl.

How do you emotionally separate from your mother and change? Work on your issues about your mother and men in psychotherapy. Develop friendships with older women who can be role models and mentors. Read self-help books. Observe the behavior of other women who have healthy relationships with men. Just become more aware of your behavior rather than unconsciously acting out your mother's behavior and repeating history.

Being different from Mom is a way of moving on and separating from her and it could bring up all sorts of feelings of loss and love for your mother. You may have to grieve and mourn the loss of your childhood bond with your mother. Leaving your mother behind can be very heart wrenching, but it's the emotional work you may have to do to move on and change so that you can have a successful love relationship with a man.

Working on emotional separation from your mother does not mean you love her any less. It just means you are less symbiotic and enmeshed in each other's problems. In fact, you can have an even more loving relationship with her because you are more objective. Although I am more emotionally separate from my mother now than I was in my twenties, I currently have a close relationship with her and she is a big part of my support system.

Remember, it's been only recently that women have become financially independent. Historically, women needed men for financial survival and would stay with men under any circumstances, so the problem of clinging to an unhealthy relationship might be generational. Therefore, learning new behaviors is not really abandoning our mothers. It is making it possible for our daughters, nieces, granddaughters, and all the women of future generations to have emotionally healthier, less painful, more gratifying relationships with men.

SIX

Things You Think That Keep You Hooked on Him

Sometimes the way a woman thinks about a man can keep her overly preoccupied, making it harder for her to let go when the relationship is over.

Idealizing Him

One recurring problem is idealizing an ex—thinking he is perfect and unique—and attributing magical qualities to him. If you are ruminating about how incredibly great he is, and how you'll never find such a perfect specimen of a man again, you'll never be able to let go and move on. Try being realistic about him—focus on his flaws if necessary. Otherwise, letting go will be a never-ending struggle.

When they first met, Brian told Karen he was separated from his wife, but then never brought the subject up again. One Saturday night, Brian was acting strange.

Finally, after a few glasses of wine and Karen's prodding, Brian confessed that he was thinking of reconciling with his wife. Karen was devastated. They saw each other a few more times, but eventually Brian moved back home. Karen never heard from him again. She forced herself to start dating, but continued to compare every new man to Brian. After about a year, she came to see me because she felt she was letting opportunities with interesting men pass by because of her inability to stop thinking about Brian.

✍ Writing Exercises

• What is it about him that you think is so special or unique?

• Describe the magical feeling you get with him that you don't think you will ever get with another man.

• Describe the qualities he has that you love so much. List each and every one of them.

• Have you ever known another man who had some of the qualities your ex possesses for whom you might have had similar feelings? Describe him and his qualities.

• Are there men in your present life who have some of the qualities your ex possesses that you find attractive? Name them.

• Can you imagine yourself with another man with whom you could feel incredible chemistry? If so, describe which of his traits you are drawn to.

• Does the man you are idealizing (your ex) have any faults? List every one.

• Has the man you idealize hurt you? If so, describe what happened.

Last Ride

If you are thinking about how your ex was your last chance to ride off on a white horse with Prince Charming, you are setting yourself up for ongoing pain.

Thinking you will never meet another man for whom you feel the passion or chemistry that you did with your ex will naturally make it harder for you to let go. Thinking he was your last chance for love will make you hang on to his ankles (literally or figuratively) as he's walking out the door.

Your *must* believe you will find love again. I have had many patients terrified they will never fall in love again, only to find themselves attracted to someone new when they finally let go of their exes. Letting go opens up new doors.

There are no excuses about being over thirty-five or forty and the small possibility of ever finding a mate! Thousands of women over forty get married and start families.

When Brian stopped seeing Karen, she was forty-three and terrified that she'd missed her last chance to have a family—her last chance to find true happiness with a man. But with therapy, and her support group, she made up her mind to give herself and life more of a chance. She joined a dating service, started doing the personal ads, and attended more social functions through her work. Within two months she met a new man she felt incredible chemistry with, and who also wanted to start a family.

✒ Writing Exercises

If you are thinking this is your last chance for love (the *last ride*), answer these questions:

• Have you had an exciting relationship before this man? If so, describe it here.

• If you were in love with a man before this relationship, describe why you think this most recent relationship was your last chance for love.

• Does your family or cultural background tell you that after a certain age, it's hopeless to find love again?

• If you are feeling particularly hopeless, describe how this feels. What are the reasons behind your feelings of hopelessness?

• If your friend were in the same situation, what would you tell her? Would you be more hopeful for her than you are for yourself?

• List five people you know who have found love after age forty. Include celebrities if you'd like.

Romanticizing

Another way of thinking that keeps you hooked on an ex is *romanticizing*. As I discussed earlier, it is important to get in touch with feelings of yearning and longing as part of the process of letting go. But some women have a tendency to yearn endlessly. They don't know when to stop. It can become masochistic after a while to continue fantasizing about his coming back to you.

Sometimes romanticizing is culturally encouraged—listen to all the love songs in which women proclaim they can't survive without love. They will do anything to have their man stay with them. While there is nothing like a good romantic song or movie to get you in touch with your feelings, the gruesome reality is that some women have destroyed their lives for the sake of romantic love. Sometimes being romantic is more about desperate hope than about reality. It becomes an escape from the reality that the relationship is really over.

Michelle spent a year writing letters and daydreaming about a man she rarely saw. She was twenty-eight when she met and began dating Dan, a mechanical engineer. After they had dated a month, Dan got a promotion and a transfer to his company's branch in the Middle East. When he left, Dan told Michelle he would write and try to come back for Christmas. He wrote once a month. By contrast, Michelle wrote almost a hundred letters to him in a year. Michelle was an artist, an imaginative woman with a rich fantasy life. She spent hours daydreaming about Dan and about their eventually living together. Another man asked her out, but although she found him attractive, she turned him down thinking she should stay devoted to Dan. She came to see me when she got a letter from Dan telling her he was marrying a woman he'd met at this job. She was angry with herself and with Dan for wasting a year of her life.

Round-the-clock fantasizing and daydreaming about a happy romantic reunion with a man who is not there for you is not productive. Being in a constant state of yearning makes you unavailable to meet new men or open yourself to new experiences. If you don't eventually begin to have new experiences, you keep clinging to the past. Instead, take the energy of the romantic hope that he will come back and channel it into the belief you will meet someone new.

✎ Writing Exercises

If you are being too romantic to let go, answer these questions:

• Are you very romantic in general (e.g., you read romance novels, listen to mushy music, love romantic movies . . .)?

• What caused the end of the relationship?

• Being brutally honest, write about the realistic chances of your getting back together.

• Would you advise a friend to keep waiting under the circumstances you are currently going through?

• Do you spend an incredible amount of time daydreaming and fantasizing about men and relationships? How many hours? Does it interfere with your work or daily life?

• Do you spend more time daydreaming about your boyfriend than actually being with him?

• List the ways you think you may be denying reality and romanticizing the situation. Be honest.

Thinking About the Past

Sometimes, in relationships, we do or say things we wish we hadn't. If you keep thinking about what you might have done to contribute to your no longer being together, you will drive yourself insane. You cannot undo what has been done. Perhaps you made a mistake, but you are human and humans are imperfect. Instead of obsessing about the past and what you've done wrong, focus on learning to forgive yourself.

Do not call him to try to undo it! You will just make matters worse, because you may be rejected again, leading to another "I shouldn't have done that!" Unfortunately we cannot reverse things that have happened in the past. Learn from the experience and move on.

✒ Writing Exercises

Trying to undo what's been done:

• What did you do that you regret?

• If you could go back in time, how would you have done things differently?

• Do you really think that what you did was so detrimental to your relationship? Why?

• Do you have a hard time forgiving yourself? Why?

• What steps can you take to forgive yourself now?

If Only . . .

You keep obsessing about the events that led to the end or deterioration of the relationship. You keep thinking and thinking about how things could have been different and had a happier ending. If only . . . if only . . . if only . . . You must accept the way life played itself out. You can make changes in your future with what you've learned from the experience, but focusing on the past will only make you frustrated and unhappy.

Obsessing about him and the past is a way of controlling your feelings. You don't want to feel the pain of the loss, so you obsess as a way of avoiding the painful feelings. When obsessive thoughts of the past are coming up, try to get in touch with the pain of the loss and go through the grieving process. Allow yourself to cry. Talk with someone you trust about your feelings. (Not to him!)

Don't endlessly analyze and intellectualize, trying to figure out what happened. You're just trying to control the past. You can't control him and the past no matter how much you think about it. Stop the cycle now. Don't look back!

✎ Writing Exercises

• What circumstances, which led to the end of the relationship, do you keep thinking about?

• Do you think the circumstances you described were actually the cause of the relationship ending? Why or why not?

• If you could go back and change circumstances, how would things have been?

• Now that you've imagined how things could have been different, *let it go*. Write a happy ending to the way circumstances actually occurred.

Perfect Closure

Endings are never perfect! Accept the way the relationship ended and move on. If you have any urges to contact your ex to apologize for something you said that was hurtful, or express a feeling so that you have the perfect closure, don't. Don't call that man! You may get rejected or hurt, and then you'll have to return for another perfect closure. Accept the way the relationship ended with its flaws. Life isn't a painting that can be made perfect. Life is messy and imperfect. Put your energy into accepting the situation and looking toward the future.

✎ Writing Exercises

• What do you imagine would have been the perfect ending?

• Write about the frustration of not having the relationship end the way you would have preferred.

Let's Still Be Friends

After you've broken up with a man, it's best *not* to stay friends. You're only fooling yourself if you think it's not going to torture you when he starts telling you about the other women he's dating. Why put yourself through the unnecessary frustration and pain? It's easier to forget, heal, and move on if you aren't reminded of your ex by talking to him and hearing what he's up to.

It's better to make a *clean break* and have no contact

with your ex if you can help it. If you must see him because you work in the same place or have children together, try to keep the relationship formal and focused on your job or children. Work on keeping firm boundaries and maintaining emotional distance when you do have to be in contact with him.

Maybe after you've become involved with another man and a lot of time has passed, you can be friends. I have known women who had work or children in common with ex-husbands and ex-boyfriends who were able to form healthy friendships with them years later.

✒ Writing Exercises

• Do you still want to remain friends as an excuse to try and get back together with your ex? Write about your true feelings.

• Have you ever stayed friends with an ex-boyfriend? How did it work out?

• If you have children with your ex or work with him, write about the times you still may have to see him. List ways you can talk and relate to him and still feel safe and not vulnerable to a setback.

• *There is life after your ex!* Say this out loud or to yourself a hundred times a day—or more! You have to give new men a chance. Stop comparing new men to your ex and you may find new qualities or traits in a man you thought you'd never be attracted to. You never know what (or who) is around the corner. A whole new world could open up to you. A whole new chapter in your life could begin!

SEVEN

The Ambivalent Man

Did you ever meet a man who treats you like a sexual goddess one night, then doesn't call you for two weeks? Or he takes you away for an incredible weekend of skiing and then disappears from your life? You can't imagine what you've done wrong! You can't figure out why he's rejecting you after he behaved as if he liked, maybe even loved, you. You have encountered an *ambivalent man*!

Many of the women in my group and workshops were involved with ambivalent men, making it harder for the women to let go when the relationship ended. When they broke up with their ambivalent men, the women began analyzing what they did wrong to cause his confusing behavior. They never knew where they stood with their men because of the double messages the men were always sending.

An ambivalent man's unpredictable behavior can make you feel rejected and abandoned, leading to your panicking and clinging to him. This may cause you to call or pursue him in an unhealthy way.

Getting involved with an ambivalent man makes you feel crazy because his behavior is so illogical and confusing. Since you don't understand his unpredictable behavior, you begin analyzing what you could have done wrong, going over everything that took place between the two of you. You attack yourself and feel guilty about things you said or did that you normally would not worry about.

Chances are, you've done nothing wrong! The majority of the time, it's his own issues. All you did was care about him or participate in the process of falling in love, which is enough to make an ambivalent man go haywire.

What are the signs of an ambivalent man?

- He tells you he loves you, then starts a relationship with another woman.

- He tells you he misses you, wants to be with you, but doesn't make time to see you.

- He acts sexually enthralled with you, then seems distant and businesslike the next time you speak with him.

- He doesn't call when he says he will.

- He is involved with another woman (or women) but says he wants a relationship with only you.

- He cancels dates or is consistently late.

- He stands you up.

- You have an intense conversation where you feel really connected, then he acts cold to you the next time you speak.

- He disappears from your life for weeks at a time.

What makes an ambivalent man act the way he does?

An ambivalent man can be charming, sophisticated, and intelligent, but he is usually emotionally immature. He is looking for gratification sexually, financially, or emotionally. He may want gratification in ways he is not aware of, which makes his behavior particularly illogical. If he doesn't get this gratification, he moves on, emotionally distancing himself.

This man can be described as infantile, having failed to develop psychosexually to the point of seeing a woman as a separate being. He views a woman as an extension of himself. A man like this is totally absorbed in his own needs, incapable of being sensitive to your needs. He will panic when he gets too close in a relationship. He feels engulfed or swallowed up by a woman he feels close to, so he distances or disappears to ease his anxiety.

He may be terrified of feeling needy. If he starts to fall in love and feel dependent, he leaves so he doesn't have to feel the panic and shame of his own vulnerability and neediness. He may be afraid of closeness due to abuse as a child. He may see you as all good or all bad, cutting you off if he perceives you've done anything "wrong." You may never even know what you did.

When Alice met Carl, she thought he was everything she was looking for. He was handsome, charming, and artistic. He worked as an advertising executive.

They went out to lunch a couple of times at romantic, expensive restaurants. On the second lunch date, Carl went to Alice's office, where they kissed passionately. She never remembered feeling such powerful sexual feelings for a man. She thought she was the luckiest woman in the world to find a man she was so attracted to, who seemed to feel the same way about her. Then strange things started to happen.

Alice noticed Carl never called her in the evenings, only during the daytime at her job. He had given her a home phone number, but she became suspicious and tried calling several times. He never answered—a message would always come on. After some further investigation, Alice found out it was a voice mail number! When she confronted Carl, he admitted he had lied about the phone and was living with another woman. Terrified of being alone again and of not meeting a man who she felt such intense passion for, Alice decided to continue to date him. She was waiting for him to leave his girlfriend.

He called her constantly for a few more days, then he started calling less often. He told her he was on a deadline at his job. Finally, they made another date to get together. The day before the date, he called and canceled. He said he had to go out of town on a last-minute business trip. Alice got upset and confronted him, saying he never made time to see her even though he kept telling her he missed her. Carl got angry, telling Alice she was putting pressure on him. Alice began to feel she was losing her mind with this guy. He made no time to see her, but was telling her she was putting pressure on him! He acted sexually enthralled with her, but wouldn't make time for them to get together to fulfill all this passion. She was getting strong urges to call him. She even thought about going to his office and confronting him about his making her feel so confused. She wanted to find out once and for all how he truly felt about her. But she intuitively knew this was not the best way to handle the situation. She contacted me for an appointment.

Carl was a very self-involved, exploitive man. He had been lying to Alice from the beginning about his mysterious personal life. He initially didn't give her the choice of deciding whether she wanted to get involved with a man who was living with another woman. Carl only saw Alice as someone to gratify his sexual or emotional needs. He simply saw her as an extension of himself. Her well-being was completely irrelevant to him.

A man like Carl is operating on such an emotionally limited level, he is incapable of true intimacy. He is incapable of compassion and empathy because he's only thinking of what's in it for him. He cannot be genuinely nurturing and caring. This man will behave inconsistently, sending mixed messages.

He acts passionate, yet doesn't find time to get together with Alice, which would be logical. He tells Alice he likes her, but lies to her and manipulates her. He refuses to acknowledge his ambivalent behavior. A man like Carl can make a woman want to compulsively call him because after showering her with attention, his distancing maneuvers make her feel abandoned and rejected. She panics and runs after him because she is afraid she's done something wrong, and of losing him.

Dealing with an Ambivalent Man

If you are involved with an ambivalent man and he is sending you double messages, making you crazy with his inconsistency:

- Don't blame yourself. This is his problem, not yours! Don't take it personally. Don't see yourself as rejected and worthless. View him as a person with serious problems that interfere with his capacity for intimacy.

- Don't attempt to help him get his act together. You can confront him to get your feelings off your chest, but you won't change anything because it has nothing to do with you. The only good you can do him is to encourage him to seek professional help.

- Resist the yearning to get closer to him. You are understandably frightened of losing him, but his feelings for you are probably what triggered his ambivalence, so running after him isn't going to work.

- Don't go along with his agenda. Do your own stuff. Work on the writing exercises in this book. *Let go* now. Use your energy for yourself, not for his problems. *Back off.*

- Accept his confusing behavior as it is. Endlessly analyzing him and trying to figure him out might make you feel crazy because there is no healthy logic to his behavior.

- Work on your own problem of why you are staying with a man who drives you crazy and makes you feel insecure.

- Set limits for yourself and for him on his behavior (e.g., you won't tolerate his standing you up). Stand by your word! An ambivalent man doesn't like limit setting that would require him to accept and understand your needs, which he is emotionally incapable of, so he may disappear. This is not a big loss.

- Don't bother giving him ultimatums. You want him to be with you because he *wants to* and not because of his own terror of being abandoned or because he has to be manipulated to be with you.

Alice followed these suggestions. She didn't call Carl. She forced herself to become totally detached from the whole situation and what had happened. She started the Don't Call That Man! program and also started dating again. Even though her relationship with Carl felt unfinished, she just let it go.

When Carl finally called her, she set boundaries, telling him that unless he was capable of making time to see her once a week, she didn't want to see him. She also said she would give him a month to leave his girlfriend or she wouldn't see him anymore. Carl got angry at these new limits. He provoked an argument and hung up. Alice never heard from him again. Instead of calling him and apologizing, or running after him, she continued to follow the program of letting go. She eventually met a man who was able to have a relationship and who made her feel secure and understood. Alice realized now that if she had continued to go along with Carl's agenda, she would never had met her new boyfriend!

Why Are You with an Ambivalent Man?

A lot of women who get involved with ambivalent men are focused on passion and excitement and don't notice whether a man is capable of having a relationship. They don't see his emotional limitations.

If the need for immediate gratification of excitement, passion, and drama is the most essential quality in your selection of a man to spend time with, consider the reality that many psychopaths, murderers, and women abusers are handsome, fascinating characters. They can be charming, warm (superficially), and very sexy. Perhaps handsome and charismatic traits are not the best qualities to focus on when looking for a man to have a loving relationship with!

Qualities to look for that would indicate he is *not* an ambivalent man:

- He invests time and energy in your relationship.

- He calls when he says he will.

- He is not trying to exploit and use you in any way.

- He is considerate of your feelings.

- He displays compassion.

- He is able to listen when you speak. He pays attention to you.

- He does not make you feel like you're going crazy.

A man who is *not* ambivalent makes you feel more secure in the relationship, which results in your not needing to compulsively call that man.

✎ Writing Exercises

To find out if you are involved with an ambivalent man:

• Does the man you are involved with send you mixed signals? If so, list them.

• Does his behavior sometimes confuse you? If so, how?

• Is he involved with other women while he is involved with you? How do you find out about them?

• Does he have a hard time making a commitment?

• How does the relationship make you feel? Are you secure?

• How does his behavior make you feel? Do you spend a lot of time obsessing about it?

• Does his confusing behavior make you want to call him?

• Has he ever done anything you feel is exploitive, to you or others? What are examples of this?

• Does he demonstrate an ability to feel compassion and empathy? If so, how?

• Has he ever lied to you or others? Do you think he's lying to you now?

When you've answered these questions, go over the list of qualities of a man who is *not* ambivalent. Think about whether the man you're having a relationship with is an ambivalent man. Is he contributing to your problem of wanting to run after him and call him?

There is another type of ambivalent man I'd like to mention who can't even make it to the first date. He is usually an acquaintance, coworker, or a casual friend who acts flirtatious with you, comes to your office to talk to you all the time, mentors you, does favors for you and asks for nothing in return, or looks dreamily into your eyes.

If you're attracted to him and you ask him about his

feelings, he *denies* having any romantic or sexual interest in you. You feel as if he's leading you on or sending you double messages, which could be maddening.

Often this kind of ambivalent man is terrified of intimacy. He acts out his yearnings for a relationship by acting seductive but backs off at the mere suggestion of a relationship. He is often oblivious to his seductive behavior until it's pointed out to him.

Some of these men are ashamed or humiliated by their sexual feelings because of childhood trauma, and project their sexual and romantic yearnings onto you as if you're the only one experiencing these feelings.

Some men have a lot of rage toward women and get a kick out of acting seductive, getting a woman hopeful of their romantic intentions and then rejecting her. These are the most dangerous kind of ambivalent men.

Women sometimes have a difficult time letting go of relationships with this kind of ambivalent man because he may be paying a lot of attention to her. Or she may be idealizing him, thinking she may never meet a man who has as many wonderful qualities as he does.

If you enjoy his friendship very much, you could try and continue a platonic relationship with him but you may end up experiencing a great deal of frustration and pain.

I've known women to give this type of ambivalent man time, hoping he'll change and want to become romantically or sexually involved with them. But unless they are in psychotherapy, these men usually continue to struggle with their issues and the woman's self-esteem is shot down more and more by their rejection of her.

You are better off investing your time and energy in trying to find out why you need to be with a man who claims he is not sexually or romantically interested in you.

✐ Writing Exercises

• Are you attracted to a man whom you're not in a romantic relationship with who sends you mixed messages? If so, describe him and his behavior. How does he act seductive?

• If you were to confront him about his mixed signals, what would you say?

• Do you experience frustration or rejection in this relationship? Is the relationship really worth it?

• Would it be a big loss for you to give up this relationship? If so, which is worse, the loss or the frustration and rejection? Why?

EIGHT

He's Not Going to Change!

If you think that a man who has hurt and disappointed you over and over is going to change, you must give up your *false hope* if you don't want to keep throwing away precious years of life! Countless women have come to my office insisting that with enough patience and time their man will change even though they have been let down time and time again. Unless a man goes into long-term individual or group psychotherapy with a very skilled, reputable psychotherapist *he is not going to change*. What you see is what you get. If you believe he is going to miraculously change, *you are deluding yourself.*

Some women also have a grandiose fantasy that they are going to repair their man, thinking they will change him. *This is a fantasy.* You are not his therapist.

Some women think that their inability to function without their man is a sign of a "great romantic love." But it isn't. It's a sign of extreme dependency, pathological dependency if he's physically or severely emotionally abusive to you. The reality is that *as an adult you are not* completely physically and emotionally dependent on him. It just *feels* that way.

Often women cling desperately to hopeless, painful relationships because they dread the emptiness they will feel without their man in their life. They think if they give up hope, their man will change and end the relationship. All that is left is emptiness—a bleak vacuum—which is so terrifying that any state of connection to him is worth the suffering they have to put up with. Some women are afraid that they might even psychologically fall apart if they were to lose him and would rather endure the pain and humiliation of their dysfunctional, ungratifying relationship than go through the horror of being alone.

That terrifying feeling of emptiness was there before you met him. It may have developed in your childhood when some of your needs weren't met by your parents and you felt deprived. The bleak emptiness may also be covering up an underlying depression that you may have been living with for a long time and were unaware of because of the chaotic lifestyle you may have developed to avoid the feelings of emptiness.

Your parents' inability to give you what you needed as a little girl is why you are putting up with rejecting, hurtful, and maybe even abusive behavior and hanging on to the false hope that he will change. Women who were adequately loved and nurtured as children usually leave when a man is abusive to them. They don't stick around waiting for *crumbs*. They feel entitled to a reciprocal, full love relationship *now*.

So to get beyond feeling so emotionally dependent on a man who disappoints or hurts you over and over, you need to do psychological work on yourself and heal some of your past childhood wounds. Some of the psychological work can be accomplished by mourning and grieving over the love and nurturance you never got from your parents. This might have occurred because they themselves were incapable of giving it to you because of their own emotionally deprived childhoods. Recovering from some of your childhood trauma may make it easier for you to be more emotionally independent and less desperate for love from any man who can give it to you.

If you can accept that a man who has repeatedly hurt and disappointed you is not going to change, *you must change* by giving up the fantasy that he will eventually come through for you, and then your entire life will change for the better. Acceptance of your responsibility in your choice to stay with or leave an unhappy, dysfunctional relationship will empower you and make you feel less desperate and less likely to cling to a frustrating, "go nowhere," depleting relationship. You will have more self-respect, higher self-esteem, and be more open to meeting a more mature, nurturing, less damaged man and finally have healthy love in your life.

Evelyn, a twenty-six-year-old-actress, had become romantically involved with Kevin, a thirty-four-year-old personnel director she met on a temp job. Kevin made it clear from the beginning that he just wanted a casual relationship. No commitments. Drawn to his good looks and charisma, Evelyn accepted the relationship on Kevin's terms, hoping that he would change and eventually want a more serious relationship that might even lead to marriage.

They got together only when Kevin called, but the few times Evelyn called Kevin, he acted cold and distant and told her he was busy. Devastated by his rejecting behavior, Evelyn would vow never to call him again, then she would hear from him a few days later and he would come over and spend the night. On a few occasions, Evelyn tried to tell Kevin about her frustration with their relationship, but Kevin would usually be dismissive and switch the subject. He even yelled at her one time. Evelyn often felt that Kevin was selfish and not very interested in her feelings, but because she tremendously enjoyed their sexual relationship she continued to hope that Kevin would eventually change.

One night Kevin was supposed to come over for dinner. Evelyn spent hours cooking an elaborate gourmet dinner but Kevin never showed up. He called Evelyn the next morning and apologized, explaining that something urgent had happened and that he couldn't get to a phone. When Evelyn tried to find out what had happened, Kevin became defensive and argumentative and told her to stop being so intrusive and hung up the phone. Devastated and fed up with Kevin and their relationship, Evelyn decided to try and forget him and move on but a few days later Kevin called. Apologetic and seductive, he asked Evelyn to go to a movie to make up for the other night. Hoping that Kevin had finally changed and become aware of his selfish behavior, Evelyn agreed to the date. Getting out of the shower while getting ready for their date, Evelyn discovered that Kevin had left a message on her answering machine, telling her that he had to cancel but leaving no explanation. Frustrated and angry, Evelyn called his apartment to find out what had happened and a woman answered. Evelyn slammed down the phone. Depressed that she couldn't let go of the relationship, which at this point she felt was emotionally abusive, she decided to see a therapist. Eventually, with enough support and new insight, Evelyn was able to see that Kevin was not going to change and was finally able to let go of him and their unhealthy, go-nowhere relationship.

✍ Writing Exercises

• Are you presently involved in a relationship with a man who you are hoping will change? If so, what changes would you like to see?

• What evidence has he given you that he is going to change? Has he given you verbal promises? If so, describe them.

• How long are you willing to wait for your boyfriend or husband to change? Describe the time limits you have given him or would like to give him.

• If you are continually waiting for your boyfriend or husband to change, try and examine your feelings about being alone. What would it be like without a man in your life?

• Do you get depressed often? Could your fear of being alone be due to the depression you're afraid to deal with? If you were alone and depressed, what steps could you take to recover from feeling depressed?

• How could you make your life fuller and richer if you didn't have a man and you were alone? Were you ever alone? How did you get through periods of loneliness in your past?

• Are you terrified of feelings of emptiness you might experience if you decided not to wait any longer for your man to change and left him? Describe what you are afraid the emptiness would feel like.

• How do you think you would cope with and survive the empty feeling? How do you think other women who are alone cope?

• Do you have any childhood memories of being abandoned or feeling deprived? Do you think that your childhood might be affecting your fear of being alone, causing you to cling to an unhealthy relationship?

NINE

Obsessive Behavior

You've gotten this far in this book, and you've done the writing exercises, but you still can't stop thinking about him. It's gotten to the point of obsession!

You decide you must get information on him, so you hire a private investigator to spy on him. Or you start compulsively calling 900 numbers and use all your grocery or rent money to pay for the calls. I had one patient hire a woman who claimed to know magic. Or maybe you try to check up on him by calling people he knows, or you even hire a private investigator! No matter how outrageous it sounds, it happens. Another patient spent almost a thousand dollars to have a spell put on her ex to get him back. She never heard from her ex-boyfriend again.

Lucy, a secretary in her early thirties, met Steve through a personal ad. She thought he was the man she had been waiting for all her life. He was exciting, handsome, and charming, but he always saw her at his convenience and the relationship never really progressed. After six months, he just seemed to fade out of her life. She called him and left messages, which he never returned. She went to a psychic who told her they would eventually get back together and become a couple. She waited a few days after the reading, but was becoming impatient, so she decided to take matters into her own hands.

Lucy started to snoop around and called several people who knew Steve. They didn't really give her any interesting information, except for telling her about a new bar where Steve was hanging out. She went to the bar on a Friday night and saw him talking to a woman. She didn't have the nerve to approach him, so she went home and left more messages on his answering machine. When she didn't hear from him, she wrote him a letter.

One night she came home to find Steve's voice on her answering machine. "Would you just leave me alone? Just forget me!"

Lucy was devastated by Steve's cold, rejecting message. She realized that her dream of becoming a couple was hopeless and that the relationship was over. She now wished she had left things alone so she wouldn't feel so embarrassed and humiliated. The only positive thing she could find was that she hadn't gone up to Steve at the bar, making a total fool of herself in public.

Some women think if they bombard a man with attention (letters, messages, unannounced visits) he will be swept away by her undying passion for him and want her back. This never works! You will only feel humiliated. He already knows how much you love him. You don't have to prove it to him. Following him around is *stalking* him. Calling his friends is *harassing* him. These actions will only make you look desperate and needy, which will further alienate him. He will lose respect for you and, if you continue to chase him, may even find you repulsive. You will destroy your self-esteem and feel worse than ever.

Harassing or stalking a man is like having a tantrum. You refuse to accept what he wants. You refuse to accept reality. You must accept his decision, even if it is painful and frustrating for you!

Remember, you cannot control him or the situation. He is a separate person and has his own agenda. You can only control yourself and your own behavior.

You must learn to accept disappointment. It's a part of life. You can't *demand* a man love you because you feel entitled to his love.

Getting revenge is the most self-destructive act of not letting go. You can destroy your own life by trying to get revenge. He could get a court order of protection, or sue you for harassment. You don't need the humiliation of legal problems in addition to everything else you are going through.

Remember, stalking him, harassing him, or getting revenge are all ways of staying connected to him. *These behaviors will not get him back!* They will only alienate him further. You are wasting your time and your energy.

Obsessive behavior is a cover for the pain, rage, and shame you don't want to deal with. You may need psychotherapy to help you struggle with these feelings. If you get in touch with these feelings in a safe, supportive environment, it can help relieve the obsessing. The loss of your man could be stirring up past losses and abandonments of parents, family members, or old relationships you have not resolved. Instead of obsessing about getting that man back, put your energy into *you*!

After working with many women who have had difficulty letting go, I can tell you that if you keep putting your energies into getting him back, you can destroy your self-esteem, finances, career, friendships, health, and even your life. So don't call that man!

TEN

Getting Out There Again

Although mourning is an essential part of the process of letting go, there has to come a time when you have to move on and start meeting new men. Constantly yearning for your ex long after the relationship has ended can also be a way of holding on to him. Take the hope you had that your ex would come back to you a changed man and channel it into the hope and belief that you will meet another man you will feel attracted to.

Dating and "getting out there" helps you to see that there are other available men to get involved with other than your ex. I'm not recommending you "rebound," but meeting a new man can make it easier to let go of your ex if you're holding on to his memory too long. You may also begin to actually have fun on dates and feel less isolated and lonely.

Here are some suggestions I've gathered from my work with female patients to help jump-start your social life again.

- Go to social functions that you have an interest in—conferences, organizations, health expos, classes, psychic fairs, workshops—and try to meet people, women as well as men. Women often meet men through women they've befriended or become business acquaintances with. And it's also good to develop fulfilling friendships with women who are not always so focused on men.

- Tell people you're looking to meet someone to have a relationship with. You never know who they may know who's emotionally available and looking to hook up with someone.

- Go to singles functions sponsored by singles groups or religious organizations. At least you know that the men you will be meeting are there to meet someone and not for any other reason, so there won't be any misunderstandings. Although singles functions and organizations may sound like settings for desperate, lonely people, I've known many attractive, interesting people who fell in love with someone they met at a singles function. Sometimes it's just a matter of being at the right place at the right time. The man of your dreams could want to check out the place you might be, but you have to take the risk to be there for this chance meeting to take place. Help fate help you.

- Get involved with sports. It's a fun way to meet new people. If you have any interest in golfing, there are tons of men out there on golf courses striking important business deals. Tennis camps

are another good resource for meeting new people, as well as the ski slopes.

• Join a health spa and work out. It seems to be a
very popular way to meet men these days. All
the exercise will help you feel better too.

• Entertain more—throw parties or gatherings at
your apartment and invite a man you're interested in.

• Do the personals—I know many women who
have met and married men they met through
personal ads. They had much more success
meeting men by placing an ad rather than
responding to ads. If you're in the throes of
wanting to call your ex, call the men who
responded to your personal ad instead.

Although there's sometimes a stigma attached
to doing the personals, it does expose you to a
lot more men than you would naturally meet
during the course of your daily life. Doing the
personals can jump-start your social life if you
haven't dated in a while. Many busy people
resort to the personals because they just don't
have the time to invest in looking for a mate or
potential marriage partner. Just be careful. If
you decide to go on a blind date, meet in a public place. Don't go to his apartment or invite
him to your place! Just meet him for a drink or
coffee, so if you don't like him, you can leave
quickly rather than suffer through an entire dinner. If you get strange vibes about a guy on the
phone, don't bother meeting him. And if you
get strange vibes in person, leave! Doing the

personals may sound a little risky, but there's nothing wrong with being a little adventurous as long as you take care of yourself.

- Join a video dating service. You get to see what the men look like before you meet them, and men who invest the time and money in a dating service are more likely to be interested in a serious long-term relationship.

- Go to parties. Book-signing parties, gallery openings, Christmas parties, birthday parties, wedding receptions. In New York City, there are people who run very large parties for singles at famous nightclubs they rent out. I've known women to meet interesting men at these parties. See if your city or town has people who run similar parties and get on their mailing list.

- Visit nightclubs. I know what they say about meeting men in bars and clubs but I know many happily married couples who met in clubs. My brother, a prominent attorney, and sister-in-law, a businesswoman and entrepreneur, met in a nightclub although both previously swore they would never date someone they met at a club or a bar!

- Get volunteer work (or paid work) with your local newspaper if you have writing skills; profile and interview successful men in your neighborhood or review local nightclubs and social events.

- Become part of a theater group or play production. There's always lots of socializing going on after rehearsals, not to mention pre- and post-production parties.

• Get hold of a computer and go online. Meeting people on the Internet has gotten some bad publicity, but there are many people who have begun relationships online that have sometimes even led to marriage.

Going online is especially helpful when you're in the throes of wanting to call your ex. You can start connecting with other people and instantly distract yourself from calling that man! The downside is you can't see or hear who you're speaking to so you don't know if the man you're talking to is really who he presents himself to be. Problems can also arise if you start projecting your own fantasies onto him.

To prevent these problems, I suggest you speak to him on the phone as soon as possible so that you are relating in reality rather than in a projected fantasy. Besides, you might feel differently about him when you actually talk to him. If you decide to speak, don't give him your phone number. Take his phone number. You can give him your number after you've spoken and feel safe.

And watch out for cyber Don Juans. These are men who go online and try to carry on more than one romance at a time. Of course they won't tell you they're speaking to other women and they pretend they're just chatting online with you. So if a man starts to act flaky and ambivalent online, it's a sign he probably has intimacy problems. Men who have difficulties relating in a mature, healthy manner behave the same on the computer as they do in person.

• Learn to go places by yourself. If you can only go to parties or social events with an escort or friend, you're limiting your chances of meeting someone new. For instance, what if you get invited to a party and all your friends are busy that night? I suggest you go anyway.

Besides, men sometimes find women more approachable when they're standing by themselves rather than when they're surrounded by girlfriends. And you're more apt to talk to people if you don't have a friend to chat with.

Going places alone leaves you free to just pick up and go whenever and wherever you want so you won't have to sit home ruminating about your ex.

When you see a man you're interested in, there's nothing wrong with going over and saying hello. Or even calling a man you've met and are interested in and asking him out on the first date. Don't Call That Man! applies to relationships that have ended or are no longer healthy. Sometimes men are shy or insecure about initiating new relationships and appreciate a woman making the first call as long as it's not the second, third, and fourth call. If a man doesn't respond to your first call, then drop it and let it go. Move on to the next man.

Knowing you have the power to choose instead of waiting to be chosen may help you feel that you have more options, which in turn makes you feel less terrified of being left when a relationship is over or not working out.

A warning: If you go to a social function and don't meet any men you're attracted to, or go on a blind date with a man you find you have nothing in common with, don't get hysterical and immediately run home to call your ex because you think he's the only one you'll ever have any feelings for. Dating is a *process*. Just because you spend some time with a man who turns you off doesn't mean you'll never fall in love again. Stay persistent and keep meeting new men, but don't call that man!

When you start dating again, continue to use Don't Call That Man! principles. For instance, if you meet a new man you're very attracted to, go on a couple of dates and don't hear from him for almost a week, don't start panicking and call him! Instead, mourn and grieve over the loss of him and the future you fantasized you were going to have together. It may have been just a couple of dates but a connection was made.

Remember, any emotional or physical separation from a man you've made a connection with, especially when you don't know if you'll ever hear from him again, constitutes a loss. Even if it's temporary and not a formal breakup, it is a loss and should be treated as such.

If you treat his lack of contact as a disappointment and loss, turn to your support system and work on your own issues, you're less likely to compulsively call that man!

There's nothing wrong with *calling a new man* once to see if he's still alive or if something happened to him, but if you start calling excessively, you can scare an emotionally healthy man away. He may think you're too needy and desperate. I know it would be great to be able to be accepted for who you are in the beginning of a relationship, but unfortunately that's not how life works. When people are first getting to know one another *first impressions do count*. Would you like to go on a date with a man who's unbathed and wearing dirty clothes? Everyone puts their best foot forward in the beginning, so he doesn't have to know how desperate you can become. Remember, he may not be calling because he needs more time to think about whether he wants to pursue a relationship with you. Not all men are impulsive. Or maybe he's busy or out of town.

Try to be patient. There's a lot of anxiety in the beginning of a relationship, so work on containing your feelings rather than acting out impulsively.

If he never calls or doesn't respond to your phone call, don't pursue him or try to get him to change his mind. Accept his rejection and move on. It's better to have the relationship not work out in the beginning rather than after you've become very attached to him. Don't start overvaluing him and idealizing him. There are plenty of men out there.

Dating and falling in love are always risks, but you can lessen your chances of another painful loss if you're more careful and selective. For instance, get to know a man better before you get emotionally involved with him. Don't fall in love with a fantasy. Be realistic.

- If he starts lying, doesn't call, or is unreliable in any way, this is an immediate sign that he has severe relationship problems. He is not going to change this behavior. This is his character. Don't start trying to fix him. What you see is what you get.

- If he says from the beginning that he doesn't want a long-term committed relationship, this is a big sign. Listen to what he says. Don't be grandiose and think you'll get him to change his mind. Use your energy to go find another man who is looking for a committed relationship.

- If he says he's married or emotionally involved with someone else, don't expect him to leave the other person for you. He may have more than one relationship at a time because he's afraid of intimacy or commitment. You don't need this kind of self-destructive love triangle. Tell him to go work out his oedipal problem with someone else.

- If he acts physically or verbally abusive in any way, leave immediately! If he hits you, is overly critical of you, insults you, or curses at you, leave even if you're out on a date! Don't worry about being polite. You don't have to tolerate any abuse.

If you have a hard time letting go, then be more careful of the men you get attached to. Remember, women tend to become emotionally attached to men they have sex with, so try to be less impulsive about acting out your sexual urges with someone you barely know. Try to work on your own need for instant gratification and develop your capacity to contain your sexual impulses until you get to know a man better. Think more in terms of the future rather than the immediate moment and "feeling good."

Just because you're wildly attracted to a gorgeous man you met at a party who's seductive and has a great job doesn't mean you have to jump right into bed with him. The reality could be he's compulsively lying about his job and acting seductive because he's looking for the instant sexual gratification of a one-night stand and has no interest in relating to a woman on a deeper, more permanent basis. If you take the time to get to know him, you can find out more information about him and prevent yourself from getting hurt.

Work on becoming more mature and less shallow in your own taste in men. You might want to think about why you get so swept away by looks and charm and the outside packaging. Try to work on developing relationships with men who you may not be initially crazy about but who are emotionally mature, considerate of your feelings, not manipulative or exploitative, and are interested in you and pursuing the possibility of a committed relationship. The kind of man I've just described may not be as stimulating as a self-absorbed, seductive, emotionally adolescent man (see chapter seven: "The Ambivalent Man"), but if you want to have a healthy reciprocal relationship with a future, you may have to do some inner work to find out why a stable, nurturing man is so boring to you.

I can't begin to tell you how many women I know who have wasted their entire twenties and thirties on men who were emotionally incapable of a healthy relationship and/or wouldn't commit to marriage and family. By the time the women had the emotional strength to leave (sometimes the men left them), they were well into their forties and concerned about their biological clock soon running out. They lived with deep regret of the precious time they felt they had lost. So it's important to do the inner emotional work on your issues about your judgment and choice in men before it's too late.

I have found in my psychotherapy practice and personal life that women who have successful relationships with men are very realistic. When they see signs of severe relationship problems or are rejected, they leave, period. They don't try to delude themselves. They know what they want. They feel entitled to love, a good relationship, and decent, respectful behavior. In general, they are very careful whom they give their hearts to.

And don't use the excuse "there are no men out there" because that's simply not true! People are getting married all the time and at all ages. It still takes a year to book a hall for a wedding. There are always droves of wedding announcements in newspapers. Yes, there's a high divorce rate but the people divorcing are remarrying again. Remember, there are lots of men of all ages who want to get married. They *are* out there.

Some women I know who married after having disappointing experiences with men put a lot of time and energy into looking for a new man. They went to dances, did the personals, joined dating services, went on blind dates, got fixed up by friends. They were out there! It was sometimes frustrating and disheartening, but they eventually met someone they fell in love with and who loved them in return.

Other women who were not as determined to find new men focused on their work, children, and/or creativity. Many of these women eventually met men they married through their work, projects, or just by going about their daily life.

Some women did not find men to become involved with but were busy living fulfilling lives. Although they were sometimes lonely, they preferred being open to the possibility of eventually finding a healthy love relationship to being involved in the unhappy, dysfunctional relationships they had left behind.

What all the women had in common, whether they met new men or not, was that they were all able to let go of their exes and move on. They were no longer involved in abusive or rejecting situations. They were all open to the possibility of what the future would bring them and had put the past behind them.

ELEVEN

Ten-Step Program
to Not Call That Man

If:

You have an urge to call a man you have broken up with, but know you shouldn't, or you are currently dating a man and want to call him, even though you know it would be best not to, **then:** Use the following program to resist that impulse:

Step One

• *Postpone* contacting him. *Stall!* Tell yourself you will *wait* at least two hours before you contact him. This will give you some time to work on yourself. There's always time to impulsively call that man!

✒ Writing Exercises

• What can you do (such as going to a movie or a bookstore) to postpone calling him for a few hours?

• Write about the urgent need to call your ex. Describe your feelings.

• Write about your strengths. Get in touch with times you were strong and determined and took care of yourself. Describe these times and where you found your strength then.

• See Chart 2 (page 121).

• See "50 Things to Do to Not Call Him" (page 126). Write down some things you can do from the list, or think of your own.

Step Two
• Get away from whatever (person, place, or thing) is causing you to have that urge to contact him!

✎ Writing Exercises

• If you are in a situation of being with someone
who reminds you of him, how can you get away?
Write down specific steps.

• How do you feel about throwing away things that
remind you of him (clothes, jewelry, books)?

Step Three
• *Distract yourself.* Shift your attention to something else, anything that will get you to temporarily not think of him. Go to a movie, go visit
friends—whatever it takes to stop your preoccupation with him.
    See Chart 3 (page 122).

Step Four
- *Remind yourself that feelings and urges do pass.* It just feels like this now. It will not always feel like this!

✎ Writing Exercises

- Was there a time when you struggled with a compulsive urge to do something, and the urge passed? What did you do?

- How do you imagine a person with a great deal of self-control would handle this situation?

Step Five
- Think of the *negative consequences* that can result from the contact. Avoid thinking of any positive

memories at this moment. Don't romanticize the relationship. In fact, think of all the negative qualities of your ex. Remember the times you were dissatisfied with the relationship with him.

✎ Writing Exercises

• Remember any previous times you contacted him. Did you get what you wanted from contacting him, or did you feel worse?

• Think of all the hard work you have done to let go of him—you will have to start all over if you give in and call him. List some of the steps you have taken to let him go.

• List some of the possible negative results that
could occur if you give in and call him. (If he rejects
you, you could feel even worse than you do now.)

• List *all* of the negative qualities of your ex. If there
were any times he was inconsiderate or abusive,
write about them here.

Step Six
• Write about your feelings behind the urge to contact him that are caused by *external events* (a
problem at work, money problems, physical illness).

✍ Writing Exercises

• Are you feeling abandoned or frightened by an external event (that has nothing to do with your ex) that's causing you to want to cling to him? What happened?

• If an event did occur to trigger these yearnings to call your ex, try to objectively examine the incident and your reaction. Describe how you feel from the event that occurred.

• What can you do to work these feelings through, rather than call him?

Step Seven

• Call on your *support system*. If you've gotten this far, and you still want to call him, it's time for you to share your feelings with others. *Memorize* the phone numbers of the people in your support system or carry their numbers at all times.

• Who is the first person you'll call if you want to call him?

Step Eight

• Learn to *tolerate* feelings and not immediately act them out. Sometimes in life you have to sit on your feelings and not do anything about them. Enduring feelings of frustration and the pain of missing him will ultimately give you the long-term gratification of avoiding rejection and humiliation and moving on with your life.

✎ Writing Exercises

• Think of times you were able to endure feelings and were rewarded (you stopped smoking or began to eat a better diet for a healthier body; you put up with a lousy situation at work, then got a promotion). Write about these times.

• Remember times you wanted immediate gratification and, as a result, things didn't work out (you quit a job and regretted it later; you impulsively spent too much money, then regretted it when the bill came). List examples.

Step Nine
• Remember to take it *minute by minute, hour by hour, day by day*. Use Chart 5 (page 124) and keep track of how many days you can resist the

temptation of contacting him. Keep track of hours if you have to. Knowing you are going to be able to mark down another day of not calling him may help you have a sense of achievement. You were able to control yourself from doing something potentially self-destructive. You were able to take care of yourself.

Step Ten

- If you've made it through to Step Ten, and haven't called him, *reward yourself*!! If you make it through a week and still haven't called him, go out with some friends and celebrate. Remember to always give yourself credit because it's hard to let go. It's a real struggle and takes a lot of self-discipline. It's hard work, so be good to yourself. *Reward* a job well done. You've earned it.

✒ Writing Exercises

- What are some things you've wanted to do for a long time, but postponed? List them here.

DON'T CALL THAT MAN!

Chart 1

Structure Time

Structure your time during the period you may be most vulnerable to calling him. Keep busy so you have as little time to ruminate about him as possible. If you have to stay home for some reason (illness, children), always try to stay busy so you'll have less time to think about calling that man!

	Planned activity	Did you get any urges to contact him?	What you did to prevent yourself from calling him
8:00–9:00 A.M.			
9:00–10:00 A.M.			
10:00–11:00 A.M.			
11:00 A.M.–Noon			
Noon–1:00 P.M.			
1:00–2:00 P.M.			
2:00–3:00 P.M.			
3:00–4:00 P.M.			
4:00–5:00 P.M.			
5:00–6:00 P.M.			
6:00–7:00 P.M.			
7:00–8:00 P.M.			
8:00–9:00 P.M.			
9:00–10:00 P.M.			
10:00–11:00 P.M.			
11:00–12:00 A.M.			

Chart 2

Activities to Help Distract Yourself

List activities you enjoy that will help you forget about calling that man! (Activity examples: reading, running, writing in journal)

Activity	Have tried activity and it was helpful	Will try this activity in the future (approximate date)	Activity helped but not enough to distract me

Chart 3

Early Warning Signs that You
Want to Contact Him

Keep track of your behaviors, thoughts, and feelings that lead to your wanting to contact him.

	Sunday	Monday	Tuesday	Wednesday	Thursday	Friday	Saturday
Week One							
Week Two							
Week Three							
Week Four							

Chart 4
Monthly Progress

Keep track of how long you can go without calling him. After a certain interval (one day, one week, one month), reward yourself for your self-discipline and hard work.

Week
One
How many contacts you made_____

Week
Two
How many contacts you made_____

Week
Three
How many contacts you made_____

Week
Four
How many contacts you made_____

Chart 5
Calendar

Check off every day that you don't call him. Reward yourself at intervals for not contacting him, and for taking care of yourself.

	Sunday	Monday	Tuesday	Wednesday	Thursday	Friday	Saturday
Week One							
Week Two							
Week Three							
Week Four							

My Support System

People I can call when I have a strong urge to contact my ex.

	Name	Phone number
1		
2		
3		
4		
5		
6		
7		
8		
9		
10		

Fifty Things to Do to Not Call Him

Do whatever it takes to distract yourself so you don't compulsively call him! Focus on something other than him!

- Stay on the phone talking to friends all night.

- Go to a CODA (Codependents Anonymous) meeting, or any twelve-step program meeting. Some meet at night.

- Stay busy with advancing your career—work overtime.

- Take a course in something you are interested in learning more about.

- Read a self-help book that gives you more insight into your behavior.

- Read spiritually inspirational books.

- Pray.

- Put on a self-help tape that motivates you.

- Meditate.

- Do something physical—play tennis, exercise, work out.

- Go to the bookstore, buy any book that interests you.

- Buy yourself new clothes.

- Go to the movies.

- Go to the theater.

- Take yourself out to an extravagant restaurant.

- Make yourself a gourmet dinner.

- Get dressed up and go out dancing.

- Write or answer a personal ad.

- Buy very expensive chocolates and eat all of them yourself (just not all at once).

- Do something that has to do with nature (mountain climbing or camping out).

- Write in a journal, or write a poem or fictional piece about what you're going through.

- Clean or redecorate your apartment or home.

- Watch TV.

- Watch videos.

- Help others who are less fortunate than you.

- Read a novel.

- Surf the Internet or chat online.

- Play with children and be open to their unconditional love.

- Take a long, hot bath or shower.

- Get a manicure or pedicure.

- Get a massage or facial.

- Get your hair done.

- Cook or bake.

- Work on your plants; garden.

- Go to a singles function.

- Paint.

- Go to the beach or a museum and sketch.

- Write a letter to a friend.

- Do a crossword puzzle.

- Contact someone you haven't seen in years and set up a lunch date.

- Take a short trip to get away for the day.

- Call a therapist.

- Go to a place of worship.

- Play with a pet.

- Go visit friends or relatives.

- Play a musical instrument.

- Go somewhere to listen to live music.

- Blast your stereo and sing out loud!

- Say affirmations (positive, confident statements spoken to yourself or out loud).

- Get out of the house and do anything to get away from the phone.

TWELVE

Surviving a Setback

Setbacks

Okay, what if you do all of this hard work and you have a setback? You give in, call him, and don't get the response you wanted or you're rejected.

- Accept the fact that you've had a setback and don't call him again. Stop now. Just do whatever you were doing to not call him. The trick to setbacks is to get back on track and continue on the path you were on.

- Call someone from your support system and talk about your feelings. Try not to be ashamed. Keeping the contact a secret could lead to another setback. Getting it out in the open will get it out of your system.

- Forgive yourself. You are only human. You are not perfect. Accept yourself. Have compassion for yourself. Try not to be hard on yourself.

- Give yourself credit for the hard work you've done.

- Have patience with yourself. Change takes time.

- Remember that change is a process! It is not linear. It's usually two steps forward and one step back.

Refocus

Use this time to focus on you (stop fixating on him). Take the energy you were putting into thinking about him, analyzing him, obsessing about him, loving him, and put the energy into yourself. Now is the time to focus on work, health, and healing.

Work

Now may be a good time to pay more attention to your work; perhaps this is a good time to put more energy into getting a promotion, or getting more training in order to further your career. If you are not happy with your work, go back to school or retrain yourself.

If there has been a hobby you've always enjoyed, think about making it your work, or at least trying to make money at it. Consider taking lessons in something you've always been fascinated with—art, music, a foreign language. Nurture a gift or talent you have. Follow a dream you've been too busy or preoccupied to pursue. Now's the time!

Health

Take care of your health now. Make sure you are getting enough rest and sleep. Eat three balanced meals a day. Take vitamins. Force yourself to take good physical care of yourself now, even if your heart isn't in it.

Eating nutritious foods and getting plenty of rest will affect your state of mind, helping your ability to let go of a relationship.

Exercise and work out. Sometimes you can exercise some of those yearnings to contact him right out of your system!

This is *not* a good time to indulge in alcohol or any other kind of drugs. Alcohol, even a glass of wine, could provoke you to start thinking about your ex and yearning for him. The alcohol in your system may keep you from containing your feelings. All of your hard work will fly out the window if you give in and contact him.

Healing

Now is the time to do some deep inner healing work. Focus on your past family issues and past relationships. Find out if there are any patterns that you may be following. Use this time to examine whether your behavior or issues from your past could be contributing to the situation you are in now, so you can prevent future painful situations from occurring.

Go to psychotherapy. Some therapists have very generous sliding-scale fees if you are having financial problems. If you absolutely cannot afford a private therapist, there are clinics that may be more affordable. There is help out there.

Use this time to nurture yourself. Do things that make you feel good. If you have children, ask someone to baby-sit for you and go out and spend some time by yourself or with friends (see "50 Things to Do to Not Call Him" for some suggestions).

If your ex was upsetting you and acting unpredictable, life may have been very exciting and melodramatic in an unhealthy way. When you focus your energy on yourself, you will begin to feel more centered and grounded. Your life will probably seem more manageable, more serene, and more peaceful.

Enjoy feeling more in charge of your life, although life may seem less exciting. Try to savor the quiet moments. While you were focusing on your ex, you may never have stopped to smell the roses. There are lots of other things in life to find exciting *besides him*. Having a peaceful, manageable life without constant crisis can be exciting because it leaves you the time and energy for so much more.

There is a whole world out there that doesn't include your ex. Go explore that world and enjoy.

Learn from Experience

I can't tell you how many women I've known in my private practice and socially who don't learn from their experience. They make the same mistakes over and over. So learn, learn, learn for the next time. Develop your insight and awareness. Don't be hard on yourself if your relationship did not lead to marriage or partnership.

Use this time to:

- Figure out what went wrong, if you can.

- Think about what you did or did not like or admire about your ex.

- Think about traits you will look for in a new man.

- Look at the relationship you had as a learning experience, a lesson. Then let go of the lesson, take the information, and move on.

Spiritual Lessons

If there is one lesson I have learned from my patients and from my own personal life, it is to let go when it's over! No good can come from clinging to a man. Some things are just not meant to be. Let the universe take its course.

Often, if you just leave things alone, life has a way of working itself out. Sometimes leaving things alone works out better than trying to force circumstances to be the way you want. Sometimes what we think we want may not really be the best for us. Sometimes when we look back on our lives, we realize that what we thought we wanted might have ended up being a nightmare and we're grateful that we didn't get what we yearned and prayed for. Sometimes if the man got away, you were better off! Be grateful, you might have been blessed.

Everyone has his or her own path to follow. Sometimes it is destiny that we travel a path with someone else for only a short distance. The next man you are supposed to share your journey with may be waiting for you, but you can't meet him because you are still clinging to your past.

Yearnings and Longings

It is most important to be in touch with the part of you that yearns and longs to be loved. Don't be ashamed of these feelings. It is very human and normal to want to be loved. There is nothing like romantic, passionate love, *when it is reciprocated*. It is by denying your yearnings and longings that you may act out compulsively, such as calling an ex or a man who won't give you the response you want.

It is by owning your longings and yearnings that you will attain more control over your life and be more open and free for a relationship with a new man. You must have hope and faith and believe you will find a man who will give you the love you've always dreamed of. As my grandmother Sally used to say, "Where there is life, there is hope." But to find this love you must remember: If he's broken up with you, doesn't treat you right, is avoiding you, makes you feel bad or like you're going crazy, then *DON'T CALL THAT MAN!*